M000169842

Library of Congress Catalog Number

ISBN: 978-0-578-19475-2

Printed in the United States of America
Albion Bradford Cardy
ABC Limited Press
P.O. Box 6837
Incline Village, Nevada 89450

www.excellenceingolf.wordpress.com

Edited by David Sims, Ph.D.
First Edition 2019

The front cover picture design, layout, and creative ideas were by Candi McCart.
Candi's website is www.candycoatedphotography.com

Excellence in Golf
Tee to Green

By DAVE CARDY
with DAVID SIMS, Ph.D.

Table of Contents

Dedication

I would like to dedicate this book to both of my parents: My father, Al Cardy, who got me started in the game of golf and my mother, Mel Cardy, who followed my golf career like only a mother could do.

Preface

The first thing about discovering your golf game is finding conviction, and then comes rhythm, balance, and patience. This book gives you a clear picture of the most efficient, powerful, and consistent swing ever explained in any golf book. There are a number of key variances in the Swing Formula from other methods, but the primary difference is in the technique used in the pivot.

The value in this book is that it simplifies the golf swing into an easy, repeatable sequence of movements with a method and technique that has never previously been explained in a way that any golfer (beginner, senior, and golf professional) can understand and put into practice.

The Swing Formula maximizes the efficiency of your body and will, improve performance, club speed, and consistency. It will also virtually eliminate back pain issues associated with all other swing methods. In fact, if there was ever an undiscovered path to the hidden secrets of the golf swing, this book has revealed them!

There is a thirty minute video that can be also viewed by linking onto the website excellenceingolf.golf The video is a visual aid to supplement the purchase of the book.

Individuals who adopt these principles into their game will hit the golf ball longer and straighter because it incorporates a swing movement that is elliptical in its rotation and has a powerful vertical drop on the downswing. The book details the foundation of the swing and includes important sections on the psychology of the game.

SPECIAL NOTES:

1. This book is written entirely from the perspective of a right-handed golfer. Left-handed golfers must reverse all of the hand and body positions described in the book.

2. If you have physical handicaps/disabilities, obviously you will have to make appropriate compromises in your swing mechanics in order to utilize the Swing Formula discussed in this book.

3. Many of the principles of golf instruction are repeated throughout this book. This repetition is intentional. The only way to learn how to play outstanding golf is by repeating good practices until they become a natural part of your game.

A Simple Approach

This Swing Formula is easy to learn. However, just as in building a house, the basic foundation of the golf swing must be stable and strong. This Swing Formula focuses on the principle movements of the backswing and the downswing and explains the key elements that control these movements. This concept is in sharp contrast to the more traditional golf instruction.

Prior to implementing the swing, a golfer must understand the proper grip, address position, and the desired setup to the ball. The address position is the foundation to the swing. All of the components of the address position are of vital importance. Properly established, they facilitate a correct swing movement.

Understanding and properly executing these principles is extremely important for an accurate and consistent swing. If the ball is addressed differently or altered (other than ways described in this book), it will be difficult to swing the club properly with consistent results.

GRIP & ALIGNMENT, ADDRESS & STANCE

Grip & Alignment

There are several critical steps taken prior to hitting a golf shot. Before you address the ball, stand behind the ball and visualize your shot to the target. While visualizing your shot to the target, align your target with something directly in that line on the ground and a few feet in front of the ball (i.e., a broken tee, old divot, clump of grass). (Figure 1) This is what you will aim for when you address the ball. While standing behind the ball, approach your stance to the side of the ball from approximately a forty-five degree angle. Before addressing the ball, hold the club in front of your body and square the club face in relation to your hands in the manner illustrated in Figure 2.

1

Figure 1   Figure 2

Squaring the club face while it is positioned behind the ball may square it with your stance, but your alignment could still be off-line with respect to the intended target. This will create several problems, even before you initiate your golf swing. However, by squaring the clubface in your hands, placing the club head directly behind the ball, and then aligning your feet parallel to the target line, you will ensure an accurate and consistent alignment toward the target.

The hands should be as passive as possible. You should grip the club fairly lightly keeping the tension out of your forearms. Tension in the forearms translates immediately into tension throughout the body. With any tension in the forearms, the chance of a fluid, free-flowing swing becomes difficult, and a loss of club head speed and control is likely.

The left hand is positioned above the final placement of the right hand. The club's grip is centered slightly underneath the life line of the left palm (not in the fingers), crossing at the fold of the index finger. (Figure 3)

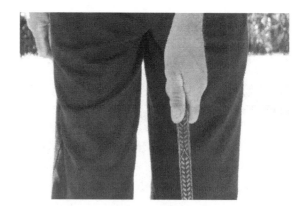

Figure 3   Figure 4

The left thumb will be about <u>one-quarter</u> of an inch to the right of center of the club grip. The "V" created by the index finger and the left thumb should be pointing to the <u>outside</u> corner of your right eye. (Figure 4)

Figure 5   Figure 6

Place the right hand on the club with the right thumb favoring the left center of the golf club grip. The "V" created by the index finger and the thumb should be pointing to the <u>inside</u> corner of your right eye. There should be not gap between the index finger and the thumb of the right hand. (Figure 5) The grip should cross <u>low in the fingers of the right hand</u> and cross the first segment of the index finger. (Figure 6)

Cock or curl the index finger of the left hand so that the last third of the index finger is touching the grip. The little finger of the right hand will be placed behind and slightly wedged between the index and second finger of the left hand. If you prefer, you can simply overlap the little finger of the right hand over the index finger of the left hand or interlock the index finger of the left hand with the little finger of the right hand. (Figures 7 & 8)

3

Figure 7 - "overlapping" grip   Figure 8 - the "interlocking" grip

If you are holding the club correctly, the left hand grip is exerting slightly more pressure than the right hand. The "holding fingers" of the left hand are the last three fingers and the thumb. The pressure points of the right hand are the two middle fingers and the first segment of the index finger. The holding pressure should be exerted on the underside of the club's grip. This type of positioning of the hands on the club could be classified as a neutral grip because it does not change the natural hanging position of the elbows. Stated in another way -- if you place both hands together, palm-to-palm, and then rotate the hands slightly to the right, you will have a perfect grip. (Figures 9, 10, and 11)

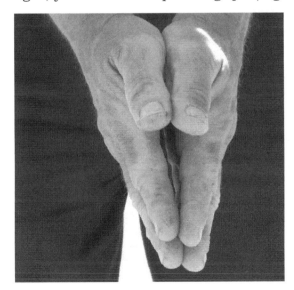
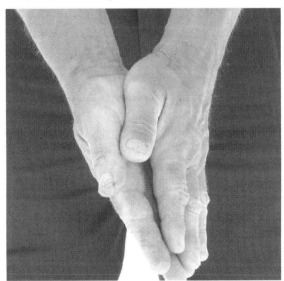

Figure 9
4

Figure 10

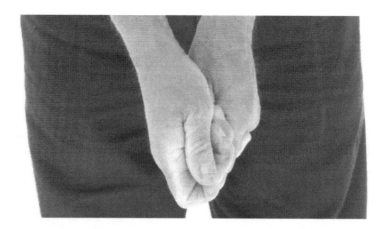

Figue11

The left thumb may be fully extended or slightly arched up. The arched positioning of your left thumb on the golf club will limit the wrist from "over-cocking" at the top of your swing. In the Swing Formula system always use a moderately extended left thumb position. The back of the left wrist is cupped. (Figures 4 & 5) Remember that the "V" created by the index finger and thumb of both the left and right hand should be pointing toward your right eye.

In golf, your left hand guides and keeps the clubface in the desired position for impact. The power comes from the right hand and arm. The hands are integrated so that they can work together as a unit.

Address

Always address the ball in the same manner for every swing. With practice and repetition this routine will become automatic. With sufficient practice you will become extremely comfortable with this procedure and this should bolster your confidence as you prepare for your swing. Developing a simple pre-shot routine eliminates the constant "fidgeting around" while addressing the ball.

Approach the ball from the diagonal angle of approximately forty-five degrees to the ball as shown in Figure 2. After you have lined up your target from behind the ball, the angled approach will help you to visualize your alignment to the target more accurately. It will also assist in setting your stance and clubface properly. Approaching the ball from another angle can make this procedure more complicated and cause indecision as you attempt to establish proper alignment and club positioning. The goal is to create and utilize a setup that results in a repeatable routine. Consistency in a pre-shot routine reduces tension in preparation for a stress-free golf swing.

While standing in the forty-five degree angle approach to the ball, hold the club perpendicular to your body and place your hands on the grip. This insures that the club is square to your hands. (Figure 2) Line the left shoulder left of the target line. (Figure 12) Now position the club head behind the ball, perpendicular to the target line. After you have set the club head behind the ball, do not look up again. The butt of your club head should be pointed toward the inside of your left armpit. Move your left foot in front of the ball with the toe of your shoe pointing between 10 and 11 o'clock. When your left foot is open (flared slightly outward) at address, it will be easier to rotate your left knee and hip correctly as you swing through the

5

ball. This will also limit the over-rotation of the hips in the backswing. At address the ball should be perpendicular to the inside of the left heel. The toes of the right foot should be pointing somewhere between 12 o'clock, and 1 o'clock. (Figures 12, 13, & 14) The right shoulder will square up with the left shoulder in Figure 14. The shoulders must be parallel the target line.

Figure 12 - set the club head behind the ball after approaching the ball from a forty-five degree angle

Figure 13 - take a small step forward with the left foot

Figure 14 - take a small step back with the right foot (the stance should be square with the right foot pointing between 12 and 1 o'clock and the left foot pointing between 10 and 11 o'clock) -- begin the swing immediately without excessive deliberation or if you prefer by starting with a waggle and/forward press

At this time the front tip of your shoes should be parallel to the target line. Visualize this as standing with both feet on one side of a railroad track. The ball and clubface are on the opposite track, pointing down the target line as illustrated in Figure 14.

When both feet are parallel to the target line, this represents what is called a "square" stance. You should use a square stance for most shots. This means that the feet, knees, hips, and shoulders are parallel to the target line. An "open" stance occurs when the left foot is dropped slightly backward from this parallel alignment. Conversely, a "closed" stance is created when the right foot is moved slightly backward, out of parallel. (Figures 15, 16, & 17) Both the open stance and the closed stance will alter the alignment position of the knees, hips, and shoulders in relationship to the direction of the target.

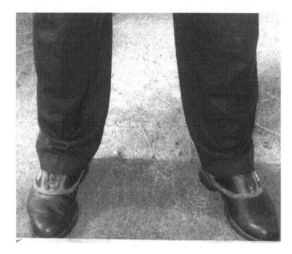

Figure 15 - the square stance   Figure 16 - the open stance

Figure 17 - the closed stance

In baseball, if a batter moves either of his feet forward or backward, his swing is altered and the resulting hit is affected accordingly – toward left field or right field.

In golf, if your stance is "opened" or "closed" to the intended target line, the ball will also be struck at an angle and cause the ball to have a different angle/pattern to the shot. Such "off-square" contact will generally result in a curved ball flight either to the right or left of the intended target line. For this reason, standing square (parallel) to your target line, is extremely important for a successful swing. An "open" or "closed" stance is used only when trying to execute a turning direction on the ball (a fade, a slice, a draw, or a hook). Using any other method to address a golf ball will cause errors in alignment and swing path.

Ball Position at Address

The ball position should be toward the inside of your left heel (for most shots). For the shorter irons you should position yourself so that the ball moves slightly back in your stance. By narrowing the stance (moving your right foot closer to the left foot), the ball position will be closer to the center of your stance. As you use the shorter clubs, the stance will always become narrower. You never really need to change the ball position for different shots. You only need to change the width of the stance. (Figures 18 & 19)

Figure 18 - a two iron position in relationship to the stance

Figure 19 - a nine iron position in relationship to the stance

8

The width of your stance may vary for the woods and be a narrower stance for the short irons and putting. The initial width of the stance should accommodate the length of the arc of the backswing. This will allow for the knees to finish even or beside one another at the completion of the swing. A narrow stance is easier to transfer body weight and pivot correctly.

Stance and Posture

When you address the ball, stand tall and tension free with your head set back in a military position (do not slouch) and held high enough that the left shoulder can rotate <u>under</u> your chin on the backswing. The left shoulder will naturally be higher than the right shoulder in the same relationship as the left hand is higher than the right hand on the grip. Your torso will naturally be tilted to the right as a result of these positions. Your head will be aligned in the center of your chest, but will also be behind the center of your stance. (Note: your eyes are parallel the target line or with your head slightly cocked a bit to the right.) This position of the upper torso is of critical importance to a consistent and powerful swing. If you do not set up in this position correctly, you will have little chance of having a successful, repeatable swing. In order to accomplish this position, bend your right knee approximately two inches laterally toward the left knee. This will tilt your torso automatically. Keep the hips square or parallel the target line. (Figures 20 and 21)

Figure 20   Figure 21

In Figure 21 note the resemblance of the arm and leg positions to a "reverse K" (the left arm and shaft of the golf club form the stem of the "K" – the right arm and leg are the two arms of the letter "K") -- see Figures 18 and 19. Figure 21 demonstrates how the head is also behind the center of your stance. This is vitally important to your swing. It is one of the most critical components of the address position.

Both knees should be flexed and relaxed. You want enough flex in the knees (approximately three inches) to keep them from being <u>stiff and straight</u>. Your body weight should be equally distributed between both feet. The weight should be evenly spread from the balls of your feet to the heels, never on the toes.

This posture angle is very important to the success of your swing. In order to establish the proper posture angle, first stand straight -- slightly flexing your knees. Too much flex in the knees will restrict lower body movement. The forward flex of your knees should place them in a line directly over the middle of your feet. (Figure 22)

Figure 22

Figure 23 - this posture results in an "ape-like" hanging of the arms

Now bend from your hips until your arms break from your sides and hang straight down under your shoulder line. Your hands should be hanging slightly outside the tips of your shoes (approximately two or three inches), and your spine should be erect. After the tilting of the upper torso into the reverse "K" position, the right hand will hang several inches below the left hand. Arc your lower back upward in a weight lifter-type position (as if you are about to sit on a high stool). The bend from the waist is approximately thirty-five degrees. (Figure 23)

10

Figure 24 - maintain your head position in a line down your spine and the center of your chest -- the shaft is in line with the fully extended left arm -- the left wrist has a <u>slight arc upward</u>

At address your head must be behind the ball for all shots. This should happen quite naturally if you have properly tilted your torso in the address position. Remain steady and loose. Focus your eyes on the back, inside quadrant of the ball, but do not overly concentrate (obsess) on the ball. (Note the straight line from the left shoulder, down the left arm and down the shaft to the ball.) (Figure 24)

Your head should remain steady, but do not "freeze" your head in this address position during the swing. Your head will rotate slightly with the turning of the body on the backswing. The "top" of your head tilts toward the target as you pivot your body on the backswing. This is important to the success of your golf swing. Do not try to "freeze" your head in any position during the different phases of the swing. The correct tilting of the head is natural and accomplishes a number of positive things. The tilting of the head allows the left shoulder to rotate more accurately on the backswing. Secondly, the tilting of the head helps to create the correct swing path -- back and through the ball. Allowing the head to tilt in this natural manner also creates a great deal of power upon its release on the downswing. The head tilt also helps to set the right arm properly on the backswing. And finally, the head tilt assists in obtaining a fuller backswing. A more complete explanation of the head tilt is discussed later, but it is important to realize that the tilting of the head is part of the natural movement of the body. As long as you do not attempt to "freeze" your head position, the correct movement and tilt will be a natural result of the rotational angle of your shoulders.

The following exercise is instructive with regard to addressing the ball:
While holding a golf club with both hands in a regular grip, reach straight out in front of you at chest high toward the ball, with both arms fully extended. Now drop both arms until the back of the left and right arms touch the pectoral muscles. Bend from the waist to complete your address position. You are now properly set with the extension of the arms. Do not have any intentional flex in the elbow and

11

keep the back of the upper inside segment of your left arm adhering to the upper part of your chest and directly over the left side of the pectoral muscle. The right elbow will hang from the shoulder naturally with the upper inside segment of the right arm linked to the upper part of the chest and favoring the right side of your pectorals. This will consistently maintain the distance that the hands are from the body from one shot to the next. The left elbow should be pointing slightly to the outside of your left hip and the right elbow should be pointing to your right hip.

There should be a straight line from the left arm down the shaft of the club to the ball. This is the result of the tilt of the upper torso in the address position. The butt of the shaft should be pointing toward the inside of your left armpit. This is also very important. These are the vital check points and swing links. The feet, knees, hips, and most importantly place a club across the shoulders to check to see if they are square or parallel to the target line.   (Figures 25 and 26)

Figure 25   Figure 26

You have now completed the information on the alignment to the target, the grip, the stance, the posture angle to the ball, the position of the shoulders and arms, and the position of your hands. With enough practice these positions should be assumed automatically when taking your stance and addressing the ball. All of the components of the address position are vitally important to the success of your swing. Accurate alignment, when coupled with the prescribed address position, will dictate your swing. Additional understanding of the physics of the golf swing will only enhance and undergird the positive effects of the proper address position. The address position is the foundation of your swing. You must have your knees, hips, and shoulders parallel to the line of the target, and you must have the proper tilting of your upper torso with your head behind the center of your stance. The correct posture, the link of the left and right arm, and a proper grip are all essential components of the address.

Review of the Address Position - The Foundation of the Golf Swing

Grip --- Palms parallel -- V's created by the index finger and thumbs of both hands pointing toward your right eye -- Grip with the left hand slightly more firmly than the right hand

Alignment --- Stance is parallel to the line of flight -- This means the shoulders, hips and knees are parallel to the target line -- Club face is perpendicular to the line of flight – Weight should be distributed between both feet -- Left foot is pointing between ten and eleven o'clock -- Right foot is pointing between twelve and one o'clock

Ball Position --- Inside of the left heel -- the stance narrows for shorter iron shots -- a narrow stance is easier to transfer body weight and pivot correctly

Posture --- Bend from the waist -- Your hands should be hanging approximately in line with your toes -- Your spine should be erect – do not "hunch" over the ball -- Arc your lower back upward in a weight- lifter-type position (as if you are about to sit on a high stool

Torso --- Tilted slightly to the right -- Reverse "K" position, critically important-- Laterally bend your right knee approximately two inches toward the left knee, while keeping your hips parallel the target line - this will tilt your torso correctly

Knee flex --- Slightly bend the knees forward directly in line with the middle of your feet

Arm position --- When gripping the club, the left elbow should be pointing toward the outside of the left hip and the right elbow pointing to the right hip -- The arms should be fully extended with the upper inside segment of the left arm linked directly over the left pectoral muscle and the right arm linked to the right side of the chest -- There should be a straight line from the left arm down the shaft to the ball, with the left arm fully extended with a slight arc of the left wrist

Butt of the Golf Shaft --- The butt of the golf shaft should be pointing toward the inside of your left armpit

Head position --- Head position is in the center of your chest and behind the center of your stance -- Head position should be held back into a military position (do not slouch) and positioned high enough for the left shoulder to easily rotate under the chin on the backswing

Eyes --- Focus your eyes on the back, inside quadrant of the golf ball

THE SWING

It is impossible to break down all of the mental and physical segments that occur during the course of a golf swing. It is, however, very important to understand the principle moves in the pivot of the body. Although the essence of the swing can be explained in a few minutes, the golf swing is a lot like a board puzzle in that the right pieces must fit in the right holes for your mind to be at rest. This book provides detailed information regarding the swing movement in order for the reader to have comprehensive knowledge of the essential elements of the golf swing. Having a clear understanding of how the swing works will give the reader more confidence in building a consistent, repeatable swing.

13

The Backswing

The backswing consists of a combination of a turn and a lift. If you over-rotate, you will hit the ball from too sharp an inside angle. If you lift the club directly upward without a pivot, you will have too steep of a descent into the ball on the downswing. In either case you will have inconsistent results in your shot-making. For this reason, it is very important to understand how much to turn and when to lift in the backswing. A correct pivot of upper and lower body will result in an ideal lift and turn.

As stated above, an understanding of how to pivot correctly is the key to a consistent golf swing. There are many perceptions and misconceptions regarding the pivot. For this reason, a careful reading of this discussion of the backswing is essential to understanding the swing.

It is imperative that your body works as a sequential unit on the backswing. To have one part of your body work against the movement of another part of your body will cause inconsistencies from one shot to the next.

The arms, shoulders, and torso must work as a unit simultaneously with the movement of the hips and legs. However, the upper area and the lower areas must be coordinated, and a good swing requires a critical timing of the two. Both the upper and lower body have their own defined parameters of motion.

If you have positioned yourself according to these instructions, you are now ready to perform the principal moves of the backswing. These are the moves that separate this Swing Formula from the problems inherent in more traditional golf swings.

After you have gone through your pre-shot routine, begin the swing without excessive deliberation or if you prefer by starting with a waggle and/forward press. (The waggle and forward press are discussed in a later section of this book.) Using the forward press will help you to get into a correct pivot and a consistent rhythm from one swing to the next. The initial movements of the backswing eliminate the problems caused by traditional swings. The primary difference of this swing formula from all other golf instruction is the initial transfer of body weight. This movement is accomplished by keeping the inside segments of both arms linked and snug against the side of the pectoral muscles and taking the club head straight back by laterally shifting weight to the right foot. The "feeling" of the lateral shift is the same as taking a small step back with the right foot and squaring off your stance in Figure 14. The lateral slide is approximately three inches. This lateral motion causes the club head to travel straight back from the ball. The movement originated by the lower body causes a slight drag of the club head. The hands move back slightly behind the club head on every swing, which creates a wrist extension during this initial movement of the backswing (the movement of the left hand backward at the wrist). Keep the club face perpendicular (square) to the target line until the club head passes the right foot. Continue the backswing movement with the turning of the hips and shoulders. The swing path is determined by the turning angle of the shoulders and is set into the proper rotary motion by the lateral slide of the lower body. This results in a swing path that is fairly upright. The left shoulder works in the same way as the hub on a wheel.

14

Figure 27 – illustrates the downward curve of the spine

The left shoulder rotates downward and then laterally to the right. At the top of the backswing the <u>proper amount of downward tilt</u> of the shoulders feels and looks like (from the golfer's perspective) that the left shoulder is pointing directly at the ball. This is an important key to maintaining the optimal swing plane and in generating club speed through impact. (Figure 27)

The rotation of the upper body and lower body must be coordinated into a unified movement. You should never "fan" the club backward with your hands, as occurs when opening a door. This fanning can happen when starting the backswing with an immediate turning motion of the hips. This causes the club to cut too sharply inside as it is drawn away from the ball. Nor should the shoulders turn in a flat manner nor parallel to the ground. With the proper initiation of the backswing the hands will be inside of the club head until the club head passes the right foot. (Figure 28)

Figure 28

Take the club head straight back by laterally shifting weight to the right foot (Figure 29)

Figure 29

During the backswing, your body weight should never shift to the outside of the right foot nor excessively to the inside of the right foot. Weight should be distributed squarely down the center of the right foot and favoring the right heel. During the course of the backswing, always maintain the original angle and flex in the right knee as shown in Figures 24 and 36. However, on more full backswings there may be a <u>straightening</u> of the right leg.

16

Figure 30

The right knee and correct position of the right hip are very important elements in a sound backswing. However, you must avoid the sway. For instance, whenever a golfer does not correctly pivot, there will be a tendency to let the right knee buckle outward - that is, to the right. This causes excessive lateral movement of the upper body and head movement. This "sway" will prevent you from being able to return the club head squarely to the ball. This faulty movement typically results in a slice, block, or cut to the right, depending on the magnitude of the "sway".

Another common mistake is the turning of the hips too sharply as already mentioned. This immediate turning movement of the hips usually results in the right leg increasing its inward angle toward the target line. It will transfer your weight and balance point incorrectly forward. These problem movements often result in a hook, pull, block, cut or draw. In the errors described above, squaring the clubface at impact is not only difficult, but failing to square the club head contributes to numerous inconsistencies.

It is very important to maintain the <u>original angle</u> of the right leg throughout the backswing movement.

Checkpoints

The first movement of the upper and lower body-pivot changes the balance of your body weight from equal balance in the address position to the majority of weight and the balance point to the right foot at the top of the backswing. On the initial movement of the downswing the majority of body weight and the balance point will shift to the left foot. The lower body moves and transfers weight as the upper body rotates. The trunk rotates around the spine as an axis. The hands, arms and shoulders must move in sequence with the transfer of body weight back and through the ball. The larger the rotation or backswing, the greater the weight transfer to the right foot. In the Swing Formula the further the hips turn to the right the greater will be the shoulder turn. A full hip turn is complete when your belly button is facing your smallest right toe.

Modern golf instruction teaches golfers to turn their shoulders a great deal further than the hips turn, thus creating a coiling action. If you are young and supple, this method can eventually be learned. However, the older you become, the shorter off the tee you become and because of the twisting of one part of your body against the other, there will likely be occurring back problems.

The backswing should be unhurried and graceful. The backswing is a swing. The club is not manipulated into position. It is swung back. In golf you swing back, and then you swing through. You should have a moderately slow, deliberate pace taking the club to the top. Every golfer will have their own rhythm for a smooth and full motion of the swing. The swing should be stress free.

In the upper body you must keep the tension out of your hands and forearms during the backswing movement. Tension will restrict the fluid motion of your swing and will shorten the arc of your backswing, thus reducing power and distance.

During the early stages of the backswing there is no visible, independent action of the hands, forearms, or wrists. By maintaining the original relationship of your hands to the clubface during the early stages of the takeaway (keeping the club face square or perpendicular to the target line until the club head passes the right foot), any unnatural hand and arm rotation will be eliminated. There should never be any intentional cocking of the wrist. Your wrists will load themselves as a natural result of the right arm folding in the backswing. (Figure 31)

The link of the inside of the arms to the pectorals in the initial move of the backswing with movement of the right hip turning back over the right heel and the folding of the right arm will shift the hands and arms to the inside swing path. This basic concept is critically important initiating the swing.

The feet are flat on the ground during the start of the backswing. As the backswing progresses the left foot rolls onto the entire inside of the instep before the left heel leaves the ground. Golfers who are less flexible must allow the left heel to elevate in order to generate a full pivot of the <u>hips and shoulders</u> for a move powerful downswing.

18

Figure 31

There should not be any premature forcing, cocking, or movement of the wrists during the takeaway. Many golfers think there is something more involved in the cocking or loading of the wrists, but rest assured that the loading or cocking of the wrists is done by the bending or folding of the right arm, nothing more.

Your left arm will remain fully extended and the upper inside part of your arms will still be linked to the pectoral muscles. The right elbow remains tucked in close to the side until approximately hip high.

The "low-to-the-ground" and inside move of the hands maintains the connection between the arms and the body. When your shaft becomes parallel to the ground, it should also be parallel with the front of your body -- with the toe of the club head pointing up. The face of your club will be angled approximately the same as your back posture. (Figure 32) The hands were inside of the club head up until this point of the swing. Now the hands are now in line with the club head. At this point of the backswing the hands and arms do the most of the work carrying the club straight up as a result initial lateral shift of the hips.

Figure 32 – the vitally important <u>first check point</u> of the backswing is when the
19

shaft becomes parallel to the ground, it should also be parallel with your toe line – with the toe of the club head pointing up (the face of the club will be angled approximately the same as your back posture) -- the upper inside segment of the left and right arm will remain "linked" to your pectoral muscle and fully extended during the first move of the backswing movement until this point of the backswing

This is the "crossroad of success" in your golf swing. You must be in this position in order for the top of the backswing to be correct. Check this position in practice swings.

The shoulders, arms, hands, and chest have moved back in a one-piece unit. If the club head is pointing behind your body, you are too far inside with your swing path. Figure 33

Figure 33 - in this photo the club head is pointing improperly behind the body when the club shaft is approximately parallel to the ground -- This error is usually the result of one of four things: the rolling of your hands (fanning the club backward) during the first move of the backswing; turning the hips too sharply; a flat shoulder rotation; or an excessive angle of the right leg toward the target

If the club is pointing outside of your toe line, you have excessive vertical lift of the arms and hands (or vertical tilt of the shoulders) without the pivot of the lower body. (Figure 34) If you are able to "freeze" this stage of your golf swing in a film/video, this would be a good frame to evaluate these critical check points in your swing.

Figure 34 - excessive "lift" - the arms and hands are pointing outside of the target line when the club shaft is parallel to the ground -- This is usually the result of lifting solely with the left arm without the coordinated move of the shoulders, chest and pivot of lower body. (disconnecting the left and right arm from the chest)

After your hands have passed your right thigh in the backswing (at the point where the club shaft has become parallel to the ground), your hands and arms will continue their upward circular path to the top of the swing. The left arm will slide across the chest, maintaining a "touching connection" (upper segment of the left arm sliding up along the left side of the chest) as the right elbow bends.

In the backswing, the first of the three vital check-points to insure that you are in an optimum swing plane is when "the golf shaft is parallel to the ground" (see Figure 32). (Note that the right arm is elevated higher than the left arm.) The left arm is linked to the pectoral muscle with the right arm linked to the upper part of the chest.

The <u>second check-point</u> of the backswing is when "the left arm is parallel to the ground". At this point in the backswing (which is approximately the half-way point just past hip high), the right arm is bent and the wrists are fully cocked. I refer to this second check-point as the "nucleus" of the backswing. This check point is a combination of lift and turn. When the left arm is parallel the ground the thumbs of both hands will be pointing upward, the right wrist will be cupped backwards, the right elbow will be slightly higher than the left arm, and the butt end of the club will be pointing to the aim line/ target line. The aim line/target line is the straight line that extends back from the ball to the target. (Figure 35)

Figure 35

On the backswing your right hip is elevated, and on a full backswing your belly button will be approximately six inches behind your chin. At impact your left hip will be elevated. Your belly button will be approximately six inches in front of your chin. This concept – regarding the movement of the belly button – <u>differs significantly</u> from traditional and current swing theory instruction. It is also the key to a very powerful consistent swing.

These simple keys to the backswing will prepare your swing for repeatable movements that you can rely on every time.

A good way of understanding the proper swing path is to assume your address position with you buttocks barely touching a vertical wall. Slowly swing the golf club to the top of your backswing. The club head should <u>not touch</u> the wall at any point of the backswing.

The palm of the right hand should be facing outward as a result of the hands and arms lifting vertically up. The left arm is fully extended and the left shoulder is directly under your chin. (Figure 36)

Figure 36

The follow through is a mirror image of the backswing. The half-way point of the follow through is when "the right arm is parallel to the ground" and the left arm is bent and close to the side of your body. The third check point is when the right arm is parallel the ground and the wrist is re-cocked (on its upward move), the butt end of the club will again be pointing to the aim line/target line, the thumbs of both hands will be pointing upward, the left wrist will be cupped backwards, and the left elbow will be slightly higher than the right arm. This is a mirror image of the second check point of the backswing. (See the photo's at the end of the book.)

The maximum time that both arms can stay extended and linked to the chest before the right arm bends is indicated in Figure 32. This extension will also help to widen your swing plane arc for a more powerful swing. (Figure 37)

Figure 37

During the course of the backswing and downswing you must maintain the spine angle that you had in the address position. Do not straighten up or change the angle of your posture.

Many golfers begin the swing with the left and right arm correctly linked to the pectorals in the address, but their backs are hunched over, or they are incorrectly bending from the spine (which drops the chest forward and down). With an incorrect posture, the backswing cannot begin without excessive hand and arm manipulation. This is why the correct posture angle in the address position is crucial to the success of your swing.

Although the information so far has presented details describing the coordinated movements in the backswing, you must visualize the backswing as a completely integrated body motion.

Top of the Backswing

At the completion of the backswing, the palm of the right hand should be facing <u>almost outward.</u> The right elbow is away from the side of your body. The left wrist is still slightly cupped. (Figure 38)

Figure 38

The completion of the backswing occurs when the torso and shoulders are turned at a ninety degree angle from your address position, with the left arm fully extended. The completion of the shoulder rotation is done with the arms. The left shoulder should be directly under your chin. On full swings you must rotate your back perpendicular to the target line. Feel the right shoulder moving up and behind your head coupled with a full turn of the hips. This will increase your rotation and set the club better at the top of the swing.

Your shoulders must stay perpendicular to the spine throughout the backswing and downswing. (It is as if your shoulders are the top to the letter "T" and the spine is the stem of the letter "T".) Most golfers are not flexible enough to elevate the left arm more than a forty-five degree angle (diagonal) to the ground. This is because of the dynamics of the swing itself. Attempts to swing the club head back any farther (for most golfers) will only contribute to the improper bending of the left arm.

When the backswing is complete, the angle of your shoulder plane will be parallel the shaft angle of your address. Actually your shoulders are making a level turn because your spine angle is inclined toward the ball. At the top of your backswing the position of the arms, hands, and the angle of the club shaft should be pointing <u>parallel to the target line or aim line</u>. (Figure 39)

24

Figure 39 - at the top of the swing, the club face and the back of the left hand are approximately at the same angle

This paragraph provides a summary of all of the elements that go into the correct position at the top of the backswing: The left knee is pointing downward toward the center of your stance. The shoulders have rotated a full ninety degrees from the address position. The weight will be distributed on the inside of the ball of the left foot, down the middle of the right foot, and favoring the back of the right heel.

The wrists are fully loaded (cocked) as a result of the bending of the right arm. Your head is steady. The plane angle of your shoulders must stay perpendicular to the spine throughout the backswing and downswing. Maintaining this posture throughout the backswing and downswing is the key to keeping the shoulders perpendicular to the spine.

The first move of your backswing is critically important for consistent results. Most mistakes occur as a result of either a poor address or incorrect initiation of the backswing. Both of these variables can be controlled with very little effort. The first move from the ball is vitally important as it sets the hands and arms, and also creates the proper rotation angle of the shoulders to attain the correct position at the top of the backswing. This "top of the swing" position enables your entire body to move through the ball on the downswing in a fluid return motion without adversely twisting the muscles. This also results in an increase in directional control and distance. The swing plane of your hands and arm at the top of your swing should be in line or slightly above your right shoulder with the club face and the back of the left hand approximately at the same angle. This is the <u>third and final check</u> <u>point</u> of the backswing.. At the top of the backswing the right arm and hand must be set in a throwing position, which is similar in the golf swing. (Figure 40)

You can purchase in laser pointer from a pet store for less than ten dollars. Drill a hole in the end of your grip and insert the laser. This will help you check how accurate you keep your swing in plane.

On the downswing your <u>hands and arms</u> should follow the same swing plane created in the backswing movement checkpoints (Figures 32 and 35) or drop slightly beneath the right shoulder.

Always maintain your balance. The foundation of a golf swing is from the ground up. Insuring that you have stability in your feet and knees in the backswing is critically important to the success of the swing. This will help the stability of the upper body, your balance, and your power throughout the course of the swing.

During the swing, you should make every effort to remain relaxed, fluid, and graceful -- as totally free of tension as possible. Allow the muscles and joints to be at ease in these movements. Any tension will reduce club speed and control. Keep the golf swing smooth and flexible. Swing the club without any resistance of the twelve leverage joints of the body; ankles, knees, hips, shoulders, elbows, and hands. You do not ever want to force or try to overpower any part of your golf swing.

Prologue to the Downswing

The initial movement of the downswing is the return of the <u>left foot</u> back to its original position or flat on the ground as in the beginning of the backswing. Transfer the majority of body weight to the left foot by flexing the knees_ -- followed by the rotating the legs and hips, which is done in one continuous motion. The flexing in the knees (semi squatting posture) half way through the downswing is an important part of the transferring of body weight, and the legs and hips rotating left. <u>The replanting of the left foot followed by the flex in the knees and turn creates vertical drop and prevents hitting from the top</u>.

At the half way point of the downswing the right elbow will be tucked against the side of your body and the left knee move toward the target. The right hip drives diagonally toward the ball. (Figure 41)

Figure 40

Everything else in the downswing will flow naturally from these movements. The upper body responds to the movement of the lower body. At the half-way-point in the downswing, as hands drop underneath your right shoulder, there is a preponderance of weight shifting to the left foot.

26

Figure 41 - this photo reveals your position at the "half-way-point" in the downswing -- At this point you must have more flex in both knees as compared with the original level of flex in the knees at the address position. At this stage of the swing, the flex of both knees will have moved from the middle of your feet (Figure 22) to approximately the tip of your shoes. By incorporating more flex in both knees in your downswing, you will create what I describe as the vertical drop or "gravity drop" that will generate greater club head speed. This will also keep the club head moving down the target line and help with your rhythm and timing. There is a <u>downward pull</u> of the entire left side of your body. The additional flex in both knees will slightly lower your height to the ball. There is also a momentary, natural leveling of the hips as the left hip positions itself forward enough to turn over the left heel.

The Downswing

The start of the downswing should occur as a result of the completed "stretch" and transfer of weight of the backswing. Even though each movement has its parameters of motion, the downswing is a strong and powerful reaction to the completion of the backswing. (The backswing in golf can be related to the wind up and powerful pitch from a baseball pitcher.) The initial movement of the downswing is a transfer of body weight to the left foot. The right knee will bend in toward the ball and the right heel is slightly off the ground.

On the downswing your lower body should react in a way similar to throwing a baseball. In baseball the left side must get out of the way for the real power to be released. This is because the left side is nearest to the direction of the target.

Figure 42 - the right elbow (tucked against the side of your body) and the left knee move toward the target together -- the right hip drives diagonally toward the ball

The chest, shoulders, arms, and hands will follow this first move of lower body. The wrists will have a natural un-cocking (unloading) as the swing starts to unwind. However, as explained before, the turning of the hips is controlled by the movement of the legs. The legs turn the left hip out of the way on the downswing. In the downswing the left knee (still flexed) will return laterally to the left. After the initial lateral movement of the lower body, the left leg and left hip begin to turn out of the way -- enough to allow the arms to swing through the intended target line.

There is a fraction of a second during the downswing (while your back is still coiled) when the lower body has already begun to move. This pause is primarily the result of the transfer of the weight of the swing shifting from the right foot on the backswing to the left foot on the downswing. This movement/shift reverses the direction of the swing. <u>This is the shift of power and control.</u> These movements control the pace of your swing. They also insure that you are swinging the golf club in the absolute optimum manner.

Many golfers make the mistake of trying to control the downswing with an upper body movement first -- specifically by using the hands and arms. This feels natural, since the club is held in the hands. However, the downswing movement is started from the ground up (stable footing, powerful legs, and correct lower body pivot). Theoretically, if you could completely isolate the lower body and keep it from moving at all, you would discover that you could not hit the ball very far at all. The power and control in the downswing comes from the bottom up. If the lower body continues to rotate, you will not be able to initiate the movement of the club from the top of the swing.

The left hip sets the pace and the control of the downswing, and your legs control the movement of your hips. Golfers who possess a very strong upper body may have an advantage in moving the arms, hands, and shoulders with the quickness of a fast hip movement, but nothing more. Whenever the upper body dominates the downswing, distance and direction will ultimately suffer. It is important to understand that the upper body cannot rotate any faster than the lower body can move. On the downswing the lower body controls and sets the pace of the movement of the upper body. In order to hit the ball farther, transfer your body weight faster to the left side. Do not try to hit the ball hard rather think swing fast. This will increase the club speed through impact and greater distance.

There is a specific transference of weight to the left side when the swing changes direction on the downswing. This shifting of body weight to the left foot in the downswing is assisted by the right knee bending toward the ball. At this point the right heel is starting its lift off of the ground. The turning of the body supplies the rotational speed for club head acceleration.

Striking the Ball: Prologue to Impact Position

At impact your left hip will return to a slightly elevated position and open to the target line for the upper body to clear. The back of your left hand and the palm of your right hand will be facing toward the target. The butt of the golf shaft will once again be pointing toward the inside of your left arm pit. The forearms and hands must rotate rapidly through impact, but never ahead of the turning of the left hip. The rotation of the forearms and hands is a key component to a powerful and consistent downswing movement. At impact, the left side is firm and the left knee is nearly straight. The leading edge of your left knee should be in line with the outside edge of your left foot. The left leg must be braced at impact. The right foot will have pivoted to the instep. The right knee is pointing toward the ball, and most of your body weight (approximately ninety percent) is favoring the left foot. The right elbow accelerates off of the right hip, releasing the arms with the rotational power the hips have generated. As you are swinging the club head toward the point of impact, you are swinging past the side of your right leg. The driving of the right knee downward toward the ball (the right hip moving diagonally toward the ball) will initiate the downward tilt of the right hip, and the left hip will thrust upward and move accurately through impact. (Figure 43)

Swing speed is generated in the Swing Formula as a result of a full turn of the hips, core, and shoulders transferring the majority of weight and balance point to the right heel on the backswing; and then at impact ninety percent of your body weight is on the left foot. On the follow through, the majority of your body weight and balance point is on the far outside of the left heel. (This pattern is a mirror image of the backswing.) The hands and arms are "whipped through" as a result of this movement. In addition, by incorporating more flex in both knees in your downswing, you will create a "gravity drop" that will generate greater club head speed. This occurs because of the timing of the hands and arms in sequence with the pivot, and the dynamic transferring of the body weight from one side of your body to the other.

Figure 43 -- Impact! -- the leading edge of the left knee is in line with the outside edge of the left foot

The left hip is several inches ahead of the left foot and elevated upward. The open position of the left hip is vitally important to a correct impact position. (The open position of the left hip makes it possible for the hands and arms to rotate as fast as possible through impact.) Your right shoulder will be lower than the left shoulder at impact as it was in the address position. Your shoulders are basically square to the target line. The left shoulder is high at impact and may be slightly open. The arms are not against the body, but extended out. The right arm is still bent slightly. Rehearse this position in practice swings. This position is vital to hitting straight shots.

Impact
There is a slight outward, lateral pelvic thrust as the left hip moves itself forward enough to pivot over the left heel. This keeps the clubface rotating at a constant rate with the rotation of the body. At impact your left hip will be elevated as a result of the straightening of the left knee and the bending of the right knee inward. Your left hip will be opened (to the left) for the upper body to clear at impact.

At impact the right hand, arm and shoulder arm making the <u>final punch</u> of power, but they should never overpower the leading left arm and hand. The right hand does not rotate over the left until after the ball has been struck. The rotation of the hands and arms through impact is done by the pivot of the body. One of the outcomes of the Swing Formula is to create a swing path which has a much longer, flatter path through impact. The low point of the arc is at the bottom of the ball, not the back of the ball. The club should be struck squarely down on the ball with irons and fairway woods or struck with a sweeping swing movement when hitting woods off of the tee. You can have an outstanding swing form on the backswing and downswing, but unless you return at impact to the position described above, you will have misdirected shots. This movement is the driving force for the synchronized unwinding of the upper body and lower body.

You must remember that smooth and tension-free muscles in the arms and legs will maximize distance by increasing club speed. This is a hard lesson to learn by those muscular golfers who feel that overpowering or pounding the ball provides greater distance. The swing must be free flowing without impedance or thought.

At impact the right foot will have pivoted to the inside of the big toe and instep. The right knee will be pointing toward the ball. Your hands will be slightly ahead of the clubface. When you are practicing your swing, you will want to check to see if you have these positions correct. You will want these moves to become "second nature" in your swing. It is essential to develop a "feel" for these check points. With enough practice a fellow golfer (or a golf coach) can use these checkpoints to spot problems creeping into your swing.

The Head Movement During the Swing

In the Swing Formula your head will tilt naturally as the body turns back and forward through the swing. Your head should be centered, but when you rotate your spine, your head will also rotate or tilt with your body movement. You can also have your head slightly cocked to the right in the address, looking at the ball with your left eye with your head cocked a bit to the right and the chin tucked in slightly. With your head in this position the club can be swung back with complete freedom of the shoulders and arms. If you look at the ball out of your right eye, your head will not be in the correct position. After you begin the swing you can rotate your head (slightly) counter clockwise to help stabilize the head position. There have been many great touring golf professionals who have used this technique, however I do not recommend this technique.

Your head does not move up and down because you are maintaining the original spine angle of the address position throughout the backswing and downswing (only the flex of the knees change during the downswing), and your head does not "slide" as in traditional golf swings. (In traditional swings the lateral sliding of the head is considered to be acceptable.) With the Swing Formula your body weight is stabilized because of the nature of the pivot movement. The steady (centered) head position eliminates any lateral movements.

Don't try to "freeze" your head position at any time during the course of your swing. Your head will quite naturally tilt on its own if you have initiated the backswing in accordance with the Swing Formula.

Conversely, on the downswing your head will naturally unwind without sliding forward or moving vertically up or down. On the downswing, your head rotates back into the perpendicular position it occupied in the address position at the same time that your club head reaches the ball. Therefore, your desired head position could be described as steady (centered), but not "frozen"/stiff. Your head must be behind the ball at impact. Your head will continue rotating through the ball immediately after impact. (Note: Golfers who have a great deal of flexibility may be able to limit the amount of tilt of the head in the backswing.)

So far we have discussed many elements of the golf swing -- top of the backswing, downswing, impact positions and head positions. These topics were provided to give you a comprehensive understanding of the golf swing. Examining the golf swing is a lot like a mechanic knowing all of the parts of an automobile and how they work. With the golf swing (as with the automobile) it is nice to know whenever a problem might occur. In order to drive an automobile, you get to a point where you simply turn the key and off you go. The golf swing must become an equally habitual routine. There should be no mental "clutter" in your head. Any golfer who tries to think of any more than one thought during the swing is doomed to inconsistency and second-guessing every shot.

The Follow Through

After impact with the ball, allow your head and spine to <u>rotate immediately</u> and very quickly upwards toward the target in a natural reaction to the movement of your body. The immediate release/ relaxation of your head is extremely important. This method will allow a greater acceleration through impact and take the tension and strain away the your lower back. Both of your elbows will straighten momentarily, shortly after impact. Your clubface remains square to the target until it passes the left foot. (Figure 44) The left hip will continue to turn level (parallel the ground) from its elevated position past the left foot. The follow through is a mirror image of the backswing. The half-way point of the follow through is when "the right arm is parallel to the ground" and the left arm is bent it will start to lift off its link from the pectoral muscle. (Figures 45)

Figure 44

Keep your right arm straight after impact until just past hip high on the follow through. The initial movement of the backswing the club face stays perpendicular (square) to the target line until the club head passes the right foot. Directly after impact the club face stays perpendicular (square) to the target line until the club head passes the left foot. This is a mirror image of the backswing. <u>The backswing swing path was down and inside. On the follow through the swing path returns back to the inside.</u> The forearms rotate left immediately after the club head passes the left foot.

32

Figure 45

The club continues its forward motion - straight up and around - on the same inside path as in the backswing. The force and energy has been transfer to the right shoulder and arm turning down and through impact rotating your head toward the target. You should come up after the ball is struck, and you should finish standing tall. Immediately after the club head passes the left leg, the butt of the shaft will be pointing toward your belly button as the body is turning with the arms until the left arm begins to bend backwards, not downward. (This is similar to what the right arm does in the backswing.) At this time, both elbows will bend and point downward as you swing the club around your neck and above your shoulders.

The Completion of the Swing

On the completion of the swing the left hip turns over the left heel. When you finish your swing, your left leg will be flexed back and almost fully straightened. Your right foot will have pivoted up onto the inside tip of the right foot (the big toe). A balanced follow-through position should be held until the ball begins its descent. Hips and shoulders should be perpendicular to the target line. (Figure 46) The torso and head will be completely straight as the swing is completed. At the finish of the swing, the knees should be even with each another. On the completion of the backswing "squeeze the knee" together. Your body weight should be favoring the far outside of the left heel. The posture at the finish should exhibit ease, grace, and balance. This can be done easily if you have followed a proper order of movement throughout the entire swing. The hips should be level and several inches higher than they were in the address position. The club face will be facing backwards. Your chest will be perpendicular to the target on the completion of the swing. Your right shoulder will be pointing approximately down the target line and your head slightly angled to the right side. On the follow through the hands swing straight up and then around. On the completion of the swing the balance point is the left foot.

Always hold your finished form and balance until the ball has begun its descent. Maintaining your balance is extremely important. A finished, balanced position (free of stress) is easily attained by allowing the club to return back in the general direction of the target - almost as a continuing, natural motion. This releases any tension which has built up in the deltoid and pectoral muscles.

Use the same Swing Formula for all shots, even when you are hitting shots that you intentionally want to turn left-to-right or right-to-left. Having good balance at the completion of your swing is usually a good indicator of sound, sequential movement throughout the course of the swing.

Figure 46

Summary

Traditional instruction about the golf swing has always taught golfers to swing their hands and arms around the turning motion of the body and somehow, while in the process of making this turn, squaring the clubface down a straight line impact. Not only is precision in this sequence of movements difficult to attain, but acquiring proficiency in executing this turning motion is extremely difficult. In addition, the poor golfer who uses traditional instruction must perform all of these coordinated feats while attempting to maximize club head speed – an even more arduous task. The challenges involved in the traditional golf swing can only be accomplished by individuals with exceptional eye-hand and body coordination, and even the successful ones must invest in hours and hours of practice to find a modicum of success.

The Swing Formula makes it possible for your entire body to work together, with everything moving in the same direction through the ball. This will result in greater distance and control. A great deal of muscle twisting and wasted body motion are eliminated. Body movements are more precise and efficient. The beauty of this Swing Formula is that it is uncomplicated. It is easy to remember and repeat. With sufficient practice and shaping of needed changes at the specific checkpoints in the swing, you can develop an outstanding golf swing in a very short time.

The address positions are the only elements of the golf swing that require a sequence of thoughtful steps. During the golf swing you do not want to be over-analyzing or "stewing" about how to swing. In golf the "active thinking" occurs before you address the ball -- when you are visualizing your shot. With sufficient practice and focus on the checkpoints in your swing, the proper address, grip, and swing keys become like second nature.

When you have mastered this swing, you will play your outstanding golf like you are "in the zone" -- that indescribable mental state where you know and feel that you are in a groove and can make no mistake. The Swing Formula enhances your chances of being able to reach this level of excellence. The reason why it succeeds is that the golfer's only concentration during the swing is on the key elements of the backswing and downswing. The swing system avoids the "paralysis of analysis" that plagues all golfers.

The way you place your hands on the grip, align yourself to the target, and address the ball is critically important to the success of your swing. The correct address position is a prerequisite to a good swing.

Consistency is the key to a successful golf swing and the keys that control the backswing and downswing keep the swing consistent from one shot to the next. The Swing Formula presents a more simplified solution to attain consistency.

Knowing the ways that the elements of the swing fit together and the various checkpoints needed to evaluate your swing can make the swing correction process more understandable. This understanding allows the golfer to make immediate changes in the swing. Comprehensive knowledge of the swing movement is the key to having a consistent swing and that is why this book has been designed to clarify the technical requirements at each checkpoint in the swing.

You will no longer need to constantly "search every day" for a brand new or magical swing thought, swing pattern, or swing principle. By using this Swing Formula, golf will become more manageable and enjoyable.

SPECIALTY GOLF: DEALING WITH ATYPICAL SITUATIONS

Hitting low shots and high shots

There are two basic approaches to hitting a low shot in golf. The first approach is to take a less lofted club and make a shorter backswing by simply choking down on the grip. The second approach is to hit the same club, but play the ball farther back in your stance (slightly narrowing your stance and keeping your hands low through impact.

When playing directly into the wind, it is usually desirable to hit the ball lower and with less spin by using a less lofted club. For best control when hitting "downwind", try a more lofted club. Keep in mind that you will not get as much side or backspin when hitting the ball downwind.

There are circumstances where it is desirable to hit the ball higher than normal with a given club. In these situations play the ball slightly more forward in your stance than you would normally play. The body weight in the address position should favor the right foot. Stay behind the ball at impact.

Hitting shots from "tight" or bare lies

On a tight lie, it takes a little more effort to get the club head under the ball. In order to accomplish this, it is important to hit down and then quickly to hit up on the follow through. In this context think of hitting a ball off of a steel plate. The club head will not penetrate the hard surface, and the ball must certainly not be hit "thin".

Hitting shots out of the rough

If the ball is sitting "up" (on top of deep grass or other natural material) in the rough, the ball will generally fly out "hotter" and with less spin. Therefore, you should use less (more lofted) club than you normally would for the given distance.

Conversely, if the ball is sitting "down," (deep in the grass) take more club than usual and hit down and then up in order to get the ball out of the deep rough. In most instances, when the ball is sitting down in the rough it will not travel nearly as far as it travels when hit in the fairway.

In a situation where the ball is "down" and in the rough near the green, treat the shot as if it were a greenside sand shot and play it as an "explosion shot" out of the grass.

Handling difficult shots

The Swing Formula provides a consistent, simple approach to all golf shots. It applies to drives, all wood shots, irons, and chipping & pitching. Shot-making is always a matter of proper address position and alignment to the target -- coupled with the critically important key elements of the backswing and the downswing. When confronted with the challenge of hitting a golf shot, simply trust the Swing Formula you have developed, be confident, and have a clear vision of your intended shot. Then execute with a relaxed, smooth, unhurried tempo. Frustration comes from having to deal with too many thoughts - too much fear, doubt, and negative thinking.

Analyzing Ball Flight

One of the major variables affecting desired ball flight is improper alignment. Care must always be taken to incorporate alignment as a part of your initial, pre-shot routine. Improper alignment with respect to your intended ball flight will always affect your shot results. Alignment is as important as a good swing.

The correct swing path is "slightly down (low-to-the-ground) and inside" on the backswing and straight toward the target through impact (the target is square to your swing path) -- and then up and around your neck and above your shoulders on the follow-through. If you do this correctly (and you have been diligent in your alignment and address position), you should have good results with your shots flying directly at your target.

However, if you aligned your stance to the target correctly, but took the club down and through the ball in an outward direction (right of the target line) instead of at the target line (square to the swing plane arc), the ball will start out to the right and will travel either straight right or turn left or turn right after the ball has begun its initial direction to the right. (Figure 47) The cause of this erratic ball flight is swinging in an outward direction with the club face square, closed, or opened at impact.

Figure 47 - the club is swinging in an outward direction with the clubface square to that direction

On the other hand, if your ball goes straight left and then turns to the left or turns to the right, you are bringing the club head down across the ball from the outside. In the instance where you bring the club across from the outside, the clubface at impact can be square, closed or open. If the clubface was square at impact, the ball will go straight left. If the clubface is closed at impact, the ball will start straight left and then turn farther left. If the clubface was open at impact, the ball will start left and either slice or fade back to the right, depending on how severe the clubface was open at impact. (Figure 48)

Figure 48 - the club is swinging across the target line from the outside with a square clubface to the left

If you strike the ball and it travels straight and then turns right or left, you have swung correctly, but the clubface was open or closed at impact.

Keep in mind that the club shaft started at a ninety degree angle to the target, with the butt of the shaft pointing to the inside of your left armpit. Therefore, the shaft must return to this ninety degree position for the ball to travel straight. If the shaft is slanted back toward your right pocket at impact, your ball will hook. (Figure 49)

Figure 49   Figure 50

If the shaft is angled too far forward (pointing toward your left pocket), you will block or slice the ball. (Figure 50) Shaft angle at impact is critical to hitting a shot straight towards the target.

Side Hill Lies

On downhill or uphill lies the ball will always be addressed slightly closer toward your higher foot. For this reason, the width of your stance is extremely important when undertaking these side hill shots. It is also very important to take a less lofted club when faced with an uphill lie and a more lofted club on a downhill lie. You must make a special effort to stabilize your body with side hill shots. To do this, you must make sure that you tilt your body with the slope. This means you lean your body at approximately the same angle as the hillside. (Figures 51 & 52)

Figure 51

Figure 52   Figure 53

Side hill lie angles (with the ball angled in either above or below your feet) require that you lengthen your distance from the ball or stand slightly closer to the ball. In Figure 53 the ball is on a downhill lie, so you would stand slightly closer to the ball or bend a bit more from the hips or lengthen the grip on the club or a combination of all three. Nothing else changes except when the severity of the slope may require you to aim more to the left of the target (when on an extreme down slope such as Figure 53) or aim more to the right in a situation such as in Figure 54. In

40

both cases the ball will tend to move in a trajectory in the direction of the slope.

Figure 54- note that in this side hill lie (ball above the feet) you choke down on the grip in order to shorten the distance to the ball

Address the ball in the same fashion for all shots, whether it is a sand shot, ball in the rough, side-hill or down-hill lie. There is no need to ever open or close the clubface or stance for any routine shot.

Figure 55 - a full pivot of the right hip with the majority of body weight back on the right heel -- the left knee has a downward flex and is pointing toward the center of your stance -- the left arm is fully extended

Figure 56 - the body weight will shift to the back of the right heel -- on full swings there may be a straightening of the right knee

It is very important to understand that any attempt to swing the arms further back than the diagonal, for most golfers, will be extremely difficult and will only contribute to the error of bending the left arm.

Figure 57 - the head tilts (it does not slide) – the balance point should be distributed on the inside of the ball of the left foot, and down the middle of the right foot favoring the back of the right heel

Your head must remain steady (centered). Some golfers will be able to keep their head more perpendicular to the target line; other less flexible players will need to tilt their head slightly in the beginning of the backswing.

In order to experience this "feeling", stand in front of and square to a wall and then lean your head against the wall. (Don't do this in front of friends who already think you are "nuts" about golf!!) While leaning your head against the wall, assume your address position. Make a backswing motion without a club while your head remains against the wall. That is the sensation of the head in the Swing Formula (the head does not slide). The "steady head" versus a lateral slide of the head will also help to prevent the swing path from traveling too far inside on the backswing.

The camera angle in Figure 57 makes it easy to see that the right elbow is above the upper part of the left arm at the top of the swing. The right arm forearm should point obliquely toward the ground. Maintaining this relationship with the arms will also help to keep the shoulders tilted downward properly and keep the swing plane more vertical. This is the ideal position to maximize the power in what I have described as the vertical drop or "gravity drop", and it will give you the most club speed on the downswing.

The Waggle and the Forward Press

The purpose of the waggle (a small, back-and-forth movement of the club at address) is to get the muscles relaxed, and to give you an advantage in shot-making that you would not have if you were to start from a completely stationary position. The waggle is, to a large degree, the hand action of a miniature half swing. The waggle also helps to keep you from over-thinking and serves as a tension breaker. The waggle should be done after setting the club head behind the ball with the arms linked to the pectorals.

The forward press has a different function. With the forward press, the idea is to start the swing from a motion already begun rather than from a stationary start. The forward press should be a very slight rocking motion triggering by bending the right knee slightly forward toward the target before starting the backswing. This turns the hips marginally toward the hole followed by the lateral shift of the hips with the movement of the upper body. This little rocking "motion" of the hips gets your swing started, breaks the tension, and sets the rhythm of the swing. It is a routine that will help you to get started on the backswing in the same manner each time. It is the beginning of a leisurely slinging movement. All of these steps contribute to a smooth and powerful, rhythmic, swing movement. If these preparatory steps are regularly followed, the swing movement will become a natural part of your setup and you will maintain a fluid movement in your swing.

The golf swing has a three count tempo. The forward press is count one. The backswing is count two. The forward swing is count three. This should be your rhythm. One, two, and three -- on every swing -- for every length of club -- chip, pitch, half swing and full swings. (The "and" is the nanosecond pause at the top of the swing.)

Here is how you integrate the waggle and forward press into you Swing Formula. Begin with the prescribed pre-shot routine -- stand behind the ball and align yourself to the target. Then approach the ball from the approximately forty-five degree angle (diagonal angle) and place your hands on the grip while holding the club in front of your body – squaring the club face in the manner illustrated in Figure 2. Place the club head behind the ball, perpendicular to the target line. Take a step forward with your left foot, placing the toe of your shoe pointing approximately at eleven o'clock, and then move your right foot back to where the toe of your right shoe is pointing at twelve o'clock. The tips of your shoes should be parallel to the target line and the ball placed somewhere inside of your left heel. All of the components of the address position will be set automatically after you have squared up your right foot. (Figure 14) Next, begin your swing <u>immediately</u> without thought or deliberation or by triggering the swing with a waggle and/forward press.

Pitching and Chipping

The chip shot is a short stroke similar to a putt. A pitch shot is merely a shorter version of a full swing. In order to be successful at chipping and pitching you must adjust your stance by placing your feet closer together and choke down on the grip. This limits the distance that you will hit the ball. The ball position (in relationship to your stance) will vary, depending on the height of the pitch or chip desired. Most of these shots will be played toward the center of your stance. On chip shots you will usually place approximately sixty percent (60%) of your weight on your left foot and keep the weight on the left foot during the stroke.

Under some circumstances (where absolute control of height and distance is imperative) you might have to change your hand position to be farther behind the ball at address in order to increase the height of the shot. Placing your weight farther back in the stance will also elevate the height of the shot. In pitching and chipping, the movement and tempo of the swing is performed in the same manner as in all other swings (only the swing is shorter). Take the club back -- down and inside -- with a "linked" unified body movement. Remember to use a waggle and/or forward press. The forward stroke is done with the "feeling" that the entire left side moves together. With chipping, the bending of your left knee will be relatively small since you are only stroking the ball a short distance. Remember to keep the tension out of your hands and forearms. Your upper and lower body must work together, even on very short shots. When chipping, your right arm moves in a manner similar to tossing a ball underhanded onto the green. (Practice this movement to get a "feel" for chipping -- as in slow-pitch softball.)

With chip shots, immediately after impact the left shoulder will rotate left -- opening up toward the target. This is important because it allows the hands and arms to swing straight through and up toward the target.

Distance is critically important on all pitch and chip shots. Under certain circumstances a golfer may be forced to open up the clubface and stance to control the distance on a very delicate shot. However, this technique of opening up the clubface should only be used when there are no other options.

For distance control, you have as many types of controlled "short shots" as you have wedges in your bag -- multiplied by the number of hand placement positions up and down the grip. You can also increase your options on short shots by changing the width of your stance, changing how far you place your hands behind the ball in the address position, and varying how much you open up the club face.

By using these techniques you eliminate the need to try to hit "softer shots" by shortening your backswing or by trying to slow down your swing. The variations are primarily done by changing the width of your stance or changing how much you choke down on the club. A day of practice will allow you to begin to appreciate the simplicity and accuracy of this approach.

Pitch shots are merely a shorter version of a full swing. The distance and range of a pitch shot is controlled by the loft of the club, width of your stance and choking down on the grip. The arc of the swing will be reduced as a result of any of these adjustments. With a pitch, the width of your stance will normally be narrower. In contrast with pitching, chipping has a very short stroke. When chipping, the left foot should favor an eleven o'clock position and the right foot should point toward twelve o'clock. Your stance will be open in order to limit the range of the backswing. In chipping you will choke down on the grip since the size of the stroke is very small. Only in the rarest of circumstances will you ever open up the clubface or place your hands behind the club head to control distance. These two maneuvers usually occur in sand shots around the green or "quick stop" short shots. With chipping you want just enough flex in your knees to keep them from being stiff/straight and to keep the tension out of your legs. The shoulders will be slightly opened in the address position.

On very short chip shots the left arm and wrist will remain reasonably straight at impact and on the follow through. (Figure 58) If the backstroke is fairly long, on the follow through the elbows will bend and fold up naturally. (Figure 59)

Figure 58   Figure 59

Getting Out of Sand Traps/Bunkers Near the Green

Accuracy with sand shots (like chipping and putting) is always a matter of "feel". Only hours of practice can truly create the feel required for the various shots that need to be executed in bunkers. Nevertheless there is basic knowledge about sand shots that can be generally applied. Most sand shots require the club face to be opened. An open face also helps to control the distance. In heavy (wet) or hard sand you must hit closer to the ball. In soft sand you should impact the sand further behind the ball. A visual for this is to think of skipping the club head through the sand like skipping a rock across water. Think of slicing the peel off of an apple. Another visual is to think of the area of sand around the ball as a small saucer and your challenge is to blast the saucer onto the green. Here is a sand play caveat: one of the major reasons for poor sand shots (especially explosive shots) is the failure to keep your eyes on the sand (intended impact area). On the other hand, the longer sand shots may require a clean pick of the ball. In this type of situation you must keep your eyes focused on the back of the ball, not the sand.

How to Hook and Slice Intentionally

There are several ways that you can successfully hook or slice. The typical ways of making these shots are as follows:

In order to hook a shot, you should aim your feet to the right of your target (since the ball is going to hook) and aim the club face to where you want the ball to end up. In order to intentionally slice, aim left and then line the club face to where you want the ball to end up.

Another way to hook a shot is to aim to the right of your target with a square club face and move both hands to the right of the grip so that the V's between the index fingers and thumbs are pointing toward your right ear. From this position the hands will tend to roll through impact and cause the clubface to "close". You can accentuate the hook by taking a closed stance (if you are really trying to hit a sharp hook). For a slice, weaken the grip by moving both hands farther left so that the V's between the index finger and thumbs are pointing more toward your left eye. Aim left of where you want the ball to finish and use a square club face. You can accentuate the slice with an open stance. Another way to hook or slice the ball is to roll your right shoulder over the ball for a hook and drop the right shoulder down through impact for a slice.

Another method that is used for turning a ball is by "feel". To do this you use a square stance with the same grip as you would use for all shots and then simply close down your hands slightly at impact for a hook. For a fade or slice, open up your hands slightly at impact. In other words, when you rotate your right palm down toward the ground, the ball will hook. When the palm is square to the target, the ball will go straight. When the palm is facing upwards, it will slice or fade, depending on the degree to which the palm is turned up. You can also think of this as shaft angle. If the butt of the golf shaft is pointing toward the inside of the left armpit at impact, the ball will tend to travel straight. If the butt of the shaft is pointing toward your left pocket, the club face will open and you will tend to fade or slice. If the butt of the shaft is pointing back toward your right pocket, you will hook or draw the ball.

You have a lot of choices to intentionally hook, draw, slice, or fade the ball. It is up to you to choose which method works best for you and under what circumstances you would choose to use it.

THE PSYCHOLOGICAL PRESSURES OF THE GAME

Many golfers, golf teachers, and golf writers have stated that success in the game of golf is 20 per cent physical and 80 per cent psychological (or some proportion that approximates this). It goes without saying that to be successful on the professional tour, you must have a certain mental toughness when your

47

livelihood depends on the difference in a few missed shots and a few missed putts. However, for the average golfer, no matter how comfortable you are about playing golf, if you don't have reasonable coordination and an excellent knowledge of how to make a good swing, you are not going to excel at golf. The following maxims should help you to deal with some of the psychological pressures of the game.

• One important approach to the game of golf is to "simplify" the mental part of the game. In golf the idea that "more is less" and "less is more" applies to the mental part of the game. In short, if you want to swing better, you must think less! The problem in golf occurs when a shot does not turn out as planned. In this situation we always try to figure out what we did wrong. Golfers spend most of their time analyzing the physical part of their game. One of the features of the Swing Formula is that it vastly simplifies the physical aspects of the game. This book has described a simple system of swinging a golf club that has never been taught in this way before. It is a system that allows you to play in a natural way without constantly thinking about and evaluating a myriad of golf swing principles on how to hit the ball. In this system, the physical elements of the swing consist only of the key elements of the backswing and downswing described in the summary.

• Never swing outside of your normal comfort zone with any club. Use the same swing mechanics for your driver as for your seven iron. Only adjust the tempo for the variations in length and weight of the club. If you need to hit a longer ball, don't exaggerate your backswing -- use a different club.

• After you have visualized your shot, select the proper club that will result in your intended shot with respect to height, distance, and angle. Like all outstanding golfers, you should step up to a shot knowing exactly how you intend to hit the ball. What you visualize (see in your mind's eye) is what will likely happen for the golf shot. This is often referred to as "playing in the present". Then align your body and swing the club.

• Don't let outside forces distract you from your shot. Pretend that you are on the driving range. There are plenty of outside disturbances on a driving range (people talking, people hitting balls at the same time you are hitting, shadows moving over your ball, etc.). You may have noticed good golfers do not seem to be overly concerned or bothered by these things when practicing.

• Play smart golf. Play the percentages. Unless it is a definite "green light" situation (no pressure), play the shot for the green, not the flag. Never play for the flag in a "red light" (high pressure) situation. Typical "red light" situations would include a tight pin placement guarded by a deep sand trap, a treacherous water hazard, or deep rough around the edge of the green. And always try to be pin high on every approach shot.

• Never give up. Remain calm and execute your best effort on every shot, even if you are frustrated or disappointed with an earlier result. Visualize every shot in a positive manner. Do not allow negative thoughts to cloud your swing preparation.

48

• If you are feeling a little nervous, take a deep breath or two and slowly exhale. Whenever necessary, just grind, grind, and grind while going through tough times. Always remember to perform your swing routine. You'll be pleased and surprised with the assurance that this ritual will provide in difficult times. Let your attitude determine your golf game; do not let your golf game determine your attitude. Whenever tension builds up while addressing the ball, step away and restart the address position. In baseball the batter often uses this technique by stepping out of the batter's box. They may change their stance, grip, and other adjustments. In golf many players will adjust the stance, or take a little half swing for a tension breaker in order to settle into a more comfortable position and less tension. Remember to keep the knees loose. Locked knees can only cause restricted movements in the golf swing.

• Always remember that all swings and strokes involve a feel for distance and basic direction. Irons are designed to make your shots carry ten to fifteen yards between each club. Become familiar with the distance that you hit each club.

• Swing at the same tempo with all of your irons and woods. There is no need to increase the speed of your swing for one club over another. Attempting to "swing harder" merely serves to increase muscle tension and diminishes your natural rhythm and control. Attempting to force a "muscle" movement in golf may result in short-term results, but brute strength is not the key to the golf swing. In golf it is the tension-free, rhythmic motion that creates consistency and successful performance. Whenever you sense yourself forcing a shot or forcibly hitting at the ball, you should realize that you are at the threshold of losing your rhythm.

• There's no need to tell anyone who has played a great deal of golf that it is the short game that decides the championships. If you really want to improve your score, spend a lot of time on pitching, chipping, and putting. If there has ever been a "hidden secret" to the teaching of the optimum golf swing, it has been revealed in my discussion of the key elements of the golf swing. In addition to these key movements, you must always align yourself properly to the target line and correctly address the ball to be successful at golf. The conditioning of your mind is the key to playing good golf. Golf is a sport with constant psychological pressures and requires the ability to handle solitude. Your real opponent in this sport is your mind. Your mind can work with you or against you. You must visualize your shots, think positively, and let your inner conditioning and shine through.

SECRETS TO UNLOCKING THE MENTAL PART OF THE GAME

NOTE: Since I first published Excellence in Golf, many people have asked me if I was going to write a bout more the challenges of the mental part of the game of golf. Although I did not plan to include a major section in this book about that subject, there have been so many questions about the enormous impact that psychological factors have on golf performance that I decided to add a chapter on that topic in this latest edition. The mental part of the game involves the ability to create and maintain ideal feelings regardless of circumstances. It is the ability to consistently maintain one's focus during the heat of a round in spite of adversity. I

49

hope that this brief treatment of this very complicated subject is helpful to my readers.

NATURE OF THE GAME OF GOLF

Before getting into the nitty gritty of coping with the many emotional factors that can adversely (or positively) affect your golf performance, it is important to get a clear understanding of the unique characteristics of the sport of golf and how these characteristics contribute to the commonly-held notion that golf is 20% physical and 80% psychological.

It Is Only You

Golf is the only major sport in which successful performance rests totally on the individual's solitary, physical and mental performance. It is not a competitive sport in which the physical performance of a competitor directly affects how successfully or effectively you can physically hit or play your next shot (think basketball - where an opponent may block your shot, or baseball - where your swing of the bat is determined by the pitcher's skills and speed, or think tennis - where all of your shots [except serves] are responses to the physical placements of the ball by your opponent). In golf a competitor cannot intimidate, overwhelm, outdistance or overpower another golfer by physical strength. In golf you can only win if you excel in hitting the ball well while maintaining good equilibrium in the psychological area. This unique feature of the game of golf has many ramifications with regard to the kinds of psychological golf pressures that creep into the golfer's psyche.

Although most of the other major sports are team sports, golf success or failure rests only on the shoulders of the individual golfer. There is no one else to blame for your errant shot. The inescapable blame for any error - any mistake in the swing, club selection, any drive, any putt, any sand play - rests squarely on your shoulders. Every time you walk on a tee for a new shot, you confront all of the physical challenges that are outlined earlier in this book in the Swing Formula, but, in addition to those physical elements required to strike the ball correctly, you must handle the variety of emotional/psychological elements that may compromise your performance.

There is only rigorous individual accountability in the sport of golf... an absolute score that can be compared to par for that particular course and for each individual hole on the course. On the professional level, the system of rewarding golfers for their performance is tied with exactitude to each individual stroke. A six inch putt counts just as much as a 325 yard drive. The players payments at the end of each tournament are based on the exact number of strokes taken. All monetary rewards are performance-based. On the professional golf tour there is not a guaranteed contract for millions of dollars for a season of performance.50
(Compare that with the structure of professional baseball, football, and basketball salaries.) I am not claiming that there are no psychological pressures involved in the other sports. Obviously there are. I am asserting that the kind of pressure and the individuality of the self-imposed pressure and expectations are more exaggerated in golf.

The Rules of Golf

There are other elements involved in the individuality of the game of golf that accentuate self-imposed psychological pressures. In golf you are expected to call a penalty on yourself if you break any of the rules of the game, even if a competitor did not see the infraction. (How does that compare with basketball, football and baseball infractions?) You must know and abide by numerous rules and regulations that can cost you dearly in competitive situations, even be penalized by fellow golfers. The way the game is set up and played makes it the most fair and the most equitable sport that can be played. There is no subjectivity to the rules, nor the playing, nor the scoring systems. That is the harsh, honest system that undergirds the game of golf. Basically, you don't deserve to win unless you hit the best shots and score the lowest score. If you do this, you win.

Time Well Spent -- 240 Seconds to the 19th Hole

There is another aspect to the game of golf that places the peculiarity of the sport in perspective. That is the amount of time that a golfer actually spends swinging at and striking a golf ball in a round of golf. If you assume that it takes about 3 seconds to swing and strike a golf ball and about 72 strokes (woods, irons, and putting) to play a good round of golf, that means that in a 5 hour round of golf, a golfer spends less than four minutes actually playing the game. Sounds crazy, but you do the math. The golfer is spending about one minute out of each hour hitting the ball. In other words, he has four hours and fifty-six minutes to do what? To worry about what just went wrong (or right) and what can he do about it on the next shot. It is this large amount of time that you have on your hands and it is this large amount of time that must be used in an optimum manner if the round is to be successful. You are typically thinking about so many things that you have an excellent chance of upsetting any round that started out well. That is why most outstanding golfers say that they try to keep their focus on one or two (at the most) elements of the swing when they are walking down the fairway or prior to hitting the ball, and why they try to have their mind clear, free of stress and tension, and the body relaxed when they actually execute the swing.

When you get all of these elements about the nature of game in perspective, it is easy to see that golf embodies unusual psychological conditions in which the game is played and a fairly unique psychological framework about competition. The primary competition is internal competition that is established by yourself - your own standards and levels of expectation about your performance. What a golf competitor does is important, but nothing that your competitor does can control your next shot.

Since a golf competitor cannot physically obstruct/hinder another golfer (we don't have stymies* on the green anymore!), that leaves two primary psychological impacts that can bring major pressure on a golfer's performance - 1) the external psychological pressure brought about by the quality of the competitor's performance and 2) the internal, self-imposed pressure brought about by the golfer's expectations of his own performance. Both of these psychological pressures can affect a golfer's performance. Of the two, the second one is, by far, the most overwhelming for the average golfer. There is no escape from the kinds and levels of pressure imposed on yourself.

It is this solitary, internal dialog - this self-imposed psychological pressure that leads all experienced golfers to conclude that golf is 20% physical and 80% psychological. What is going well for a golfer and what is going wrong for a golfer can inspire or haunt their game for days, weeks, months... even years. Ways to

51

cope with this dilemma/challenge, can test the skills of the best of golfers.

*(In the early days of golf [mostly in match play and much of it on sand greens], an opponent could putt his ball and if it stopped in the path of his opponent's next putt, his opponent would have to figure out how to play "around the ball" since it was his honor to play next. Today's players spot the ball on the green with a coin. No ball placement is allowed to obstruct a golfer's next shot.)

INTERACTION OF THE PHYSICAL AND THE PSYCHOLOGICAL IN THE GAME OF GOLF

As is obvious from the earlier discussion of the nature of the game of golf, every time a golfer walks onto a tee or a fairway or a green to hit a shot, s/he must marshal all of their knowledge and all of their positive emotional energy and hit the shot in the way that they have practiced for hours and hours. Any loss of confidence, any mistakes in a proven sequence of physical elements to the swing, any caving in to negative psychological thoughts about the swing will inevitably compromise the quality of the shot. There is no escaping the requirements of having to take full responsibility for the success or failure of your performance. The proven elements involved in the physical requirements of the golf swing have been outlined and discussed in the earlier parts of this book under the Swing Formula. The psychological elements involved in maintaining an optimum attitude about the situations you face in playing golf are immediate and "in-your-face" and must be coped with each time you play a round of golf. There is no limit to the types of psychological pressures that await the golfer. It is important to be motivated and have a positive attitude, but this is difficult when you are not striking the ball well.

There is no easy answer about how to solve the myriad of psychological challenges that can confront a golfer. As Bobby Jones, winner of the Grand Slam of golf, succinctly put it, "Anything can happen." Each golfer must search and find the best way to pull out of a psychological slump.

Four Easy Answers for Getting Out of a Slump

One thing is for sure, many of the "old standby" sports psychology clichés probably will not work. Here is a list of the ones that I consider to be too superficial to provide much help to a golfer who is trying to resolve the anguish of psychological pressure:

1.   SUGGESTION: "Golf is supposed to be fun. Just have fun."

MY ANSWER --- If you have played good golf, and you are now in a psychological slump, the game of golf is not fun. You can't console golfers who are having a serious mental obstacle to playing golf at the level that they want to play. The game only becomes fun when the golfer's level of play is satisfying.

2. SUGGESTION: "Golf is just a game. Enjoy it."

MY ANSWER --- Golf surely is a game, but it is not a game to enjoy if you are constantly disappointed in your performance. You enjoy the game when you have a mental framework that ensures that you know how to perform the physical elements of the swing, can execute consistently, and have a positive attitude to go with it.

3. SUGGESTION: "Don't be so hard on yourself; you will be better off if you are not so judgmental about your game."

MY ANSWER --- Judging your golf performance is all that you do for 18 holes. How can you not be judgmental? You would be better off with some suggestions for managing this internal, conflicting golf dialog that goes on within yourself.

4) SUGGESTION: "Find your strengths and be sure to play to them."
MY ANSWER --- I don't really know what it means to play to your strengths. I assume that everyone tries to emphasize their best game. It is not your strengths that are bothering you; it is your weaknesses that are bugging you.

Other common suggestions are equally weak when dealing with a serious problem in a golfer's game: ("Stay focused"; "You've got to concentrate"; "You've got to work harder, practice more"; "You've got to have a positive attitude.") The reasons why these probably won't work is that - when you are actually swinging to strike the ball, you should not be concentrating, focusing, or thinking about anything during the execution of your swing. The ideal mental state is one of relaxed confidence with only a visualization of the shot. This state of mind can only come to someone who has mastered the physical elements of the Swing Formula and enthusiastically plays the shot, fully prepared for any eventuality.

The Best Answer

Since "anything can happen" during a round of golf, you must work on your psychological preparation for the game by building inner resources to cope with the variety of crises that surely await you. For this reason, I have always felt that one of the most essential psychological traits that a golfer needs is resilience. Resilience is a powerful word. It is a powerful concept. It is the capacity to come back again and again in an effort to be successful with what you want to accomplish. Resilience is the ability to keep coping, to keep trying, to not give up when you are so discouraged and down and out and do not feel that you can go on. Resilience is not just a word that is essential for a golfer. It is an attitude that goes even deeper and is essential for "putting that last shot behind you." Another critical psychological trait for the golfer is confidence. In fact, I feel that confidence is a pre-requisite to resilience. Golfers without confidence are not going to have the stamina to try and try again when their game is producing dismal results. Confidence runs on a continuum from lack of confidence to overconfidence. It is essential for a golfer, but it must be at the right level. You must have a wholesome kind of pride about how well you can perform and an equally healthy respect for all of the things that can go wrong. There is no place for overconfidence in the game of golf.

Where does confidence come from? For golfers it has been forged by trial and error and experimentation in practicing and in playing the game. Confidence does not come from "not making errors." It comes from making errors and learning how to overcome them. It comes from failure and recovery from failure. It does not come from avoiding risks, but from learning the kinds of risks to take In golf there is no substitute for learning to take the appropriate level of risk and being rewarded for it, and there is no substitute for the discipline of natural consequences to learn the price you pay for taking excessive risks. The confidence needed in golf is forged in an environment that allows the golfer to grow and develop in this kind of psychological cauldron. In order to gain confidence, at some point the golfer must experience some level of success. This means that you must have mastered the physical elements of the swing in the Swing Formula, have developed a repeatable sequence of moves, and have absolute confidence that this system works well for your game of golf.   That is why the physical part of the game is so inextricably tied

53

to the psychological part of the game. This is the essential part of the confidence that you must have in your physical ability to play the shots required for the game of golf.

If you are having psychological/mental problems with your golf game, the most tangible way to attempt to minimize these kinds of problems is to return to the physical part of the swing. The reality is that dealing with the physical elements of your Swing Formula may provide just the distraction needed to keep the psychological pressure from weighing down on your game. By working on the mechanics of your swing you can be deflecting the psychological negativity that can creep into your attitude about your game.

De-funking your Game

Where do you turn when the game has turned on you? There are several activities that may help to pull you out of a golfing funk.

Here are a few that have helped me when I have been up "against the wall". I do not present them as a panacea for everyone's challenges in the area of the psychological pressures in golf, but I do submit them as alternatives to assist you in returning to a level of success in the game. First of all, you must continue to play and practice the game. That sounds pretty simple, but you must have faith that you will eventually pull out of your slump (mental or physical). You will have to be your own best coach not to give up. Let's examine the options that can help to unlock mental and physical holds on a golfer.

First of all, I would recommend that every serious golfer get a quality video made of your swing - especially at a time when performance is high and the "feel" of the swing is optimum. This video can serve as a baseline for evaluating any later problems that creep into your swing. When you are experiencing problems, you can make a new video and compare the patterns in your old and new versions of your swing. Before "tweaking" any element of your swing, I would caution you to respect these priorities - experiment with changes in your swing in this order: 1) grip 2) stance/alignment 3) address 4) ball position 5) arm position 6) knee flex 7) head position 8) posture 9) torso. Next I would review the video and compare the critical Swing Formula checkpoints in the swing of the older video with the current video. This could give you some key suggestions for making minor changes in your swing and hopefully iron out your problems.

An alternative to using the video is to get a golf instructor or a golfing friend (who knows your swing well) to analyze your swing and see if they can spot any areas that may be causing the problem and suggest areas to work on. An instructor who has taught you how to play golf or a friend who has played with you for years may immediately spot an error that has crept into your swing. You must give them a chance to help you.

Next I would suggest that you "just walk away and cool off" from a failed effort (a bad shot, a disappointing decision on the course). Everyone makes mistakes playing on a golf course. You must have a fail-safe exit that allows you an escape to collect your thoughts, then abandon these thoughts for a fresh attempt at success. This brief exit can be a kind of ritual that you have secretly developed for these kinds of moments. It should be available on a moment's notice and it must have all of the elements of a calming, soothing diversion. This reflection should have a meditative quality to it where you can empty your mind of any negative, pessimistic thoughts and transform this moment into positive, successful images of the task at

54

hand. It sounds easy; I hope for you that it is. This should be part of your psychological arsenal. There are other gimmicks that you can try. I call them gimmicks because if you are truly in a psychological box about a golf problem, you never know exactly what will pull you out of it. Both of these can be tried on the practice range, especially if you think that the problem is in the rhythm or timing of your swing. The first gimmick is to find the best rhythm in your swing by practicing with a vocal, numerical rhythm that you call out as you swing. Count out loud and time the numbers that you are calling out with the pace of your best feeling golf swing. It may sound like: "One thousand and one, One thousand and two, One thousand and three," or "One and-a Two and-a Three." You will have to find the best kind of musical timing that works for your best shots and groove that rhythm to your golf swing. If it works well, the vocal part can become silent on the course, but you can still hear the rhythm when it has become second nature to you.

Gimmick number two is to try on the range to develop such an in-depth feel for your swing that you do not need to use visual cues to swing well and to strike the ball well. You can do this by practicing blindfolded or with your eyes closed. You can have a friend observe and report to you how well you are striking the ball or you can open your eyes when you complete the swing. During this blind process you are attempting to learn how you can swing and strike a golf ball strictly by feel - that is, letting your nervous system control your muscular system without visual cues.

Quick Review of Swing Formula
My final suggestion is the most rudimentary of all. You should have such a mastery of the elements of the Swing Formula that you can quickly review these sequentially in your head and determine if you can isolate the problem. Here are the steps of the quick review:

1) The first step in hitting a shot correctly is to have a clear visualization or mental imagery of the intended golf shot. This includes the height of the ball flight, the shape, the distance and the direction. You must have a clear picture in your mind of the intended shot. The tunnel vision that you want is a clearly visualized golf shot. You must eliminate distractions such as birds chirping, squirrels scrambling, shadows moving and countless other elements that exist in the golf environment. Remember that on the driving range people are talking, shadows are flitting past your practice area, and other golfers walking and talking and laughing. In practice you ignore these distractions. It should be the same on the golf course. Good players see the shot in their mind and execute it. Everything else is blocked out. Concentrate on your game, not someone else's nor on anything else. Try not to have a meltdown just because you hit a horrible shot. This game is a series of ups and downs.

2) Step number two is simpler: select the club that can perform this visualized shot.

3) Step number three is setting up the address position. This includes the grip, ball position in relationship to the stance, alignment to the target and posture. The address position always requires a step-by-step analysis to make sure that the address is accurate.

4) Step number four is a practice swing to loosen up or rehearse a particular component of the Swing Formula. You may also deploy a waggle or forward press

to kick start the swing.

5) Step number five: Once you begin your swing, there should be a complete focus on the movement, not any element of the swing.
To achieve peak performance you need the discipline to analyze your mistakes and correct them quickly. This is a major key to playing your best golf and to keeping the negative thoughts away from your game.

The Challenge

If these suggestions don't work for you, don't become discouraged. Remember... resilience. Every outstanding golfer has come up against the mental messages that can weaken their game. They are never easy to overcome. And even more exasperating to the championship golfer is the fact that, despite their enormous, previous success in the game, they may have no clue what the current problem is. That is the nature of the game.

For some golfers, I have, as a last resort, recommended that they may find some spontaneous relief from their golf problem if they stop playing for a period of time (an extremely long break is not recommended). I always insist that they set the date when they will begin to practice again and have seen instances where a planned break from the game has worked surprising wonders on a golfer's performance.

THE PARADOX OF PLAYING "IN THE ZONE"

After discussing the kinds of psychological problems that can beset the golfer, let's turn to one of the more magical areas in the experience of playing golf. Playing "in the zone" is an expression used not only in golf, but also in other competitive sports. The general definition of playing "in the zone" would be that an athlete is performing in his/her sport at a level of excellence far beyond their ability to explain. There are many psychological layers to playing a sport "in the zone." Many that we can attempt to explain and many that we cannot yet explain, given our limited knowledge about how the human brain, the human mind, human nervous system, and the human muscular system can interweave and be influenced or controlled at both a conscious and a subconscious level. "In the zone" patterns occur when a person has learned to perform at a relaxed, intramuscular level and where verbal and cognitive directions are not functioning on a conscious level. The usual "noisy" mental messages are not being allowed to interfere at this time and the nervous system (feeling) is controlling the muscular system (physical). In this state the golfer feels that "I can do no wrong". In this "zone" the golfer's level of success is as mysterious as the negative problems can be at the other end of the golf continuum. When a golfer is experiencing the exhilarating highs of playing "in the zone," it is as if s/he is not playing with a conscious intentionality of effort, but is functioning in a kind of subconscious "autopilot" that is successful beyond their wildest dreams. If coping with the negative, psychological problems can be the nadir of golf, playing "in the zone" can be the zenith.

There are possible rational explanations for what is going on, but the golfer in this state is not attempting to understand what is going on. S/he just enjoys it and hopes that it can continue unabated. The logical explanation for playing "in the zone" is that an athlete has practiced the repetitious, physical requirements of the sport for so long and has been able to combine that with a psychological state of relaxation (their cognitive skills and emotional strengths have merged), so that this golfer is able to swing the club and play the game with minimum effort and no fear.

The fascinating aspect of a person playing the game of golf "in the zone" is that the golfer cannot tell another person what triggered this delightful state of affairs nor can they possibly guess how long it will last. They only know when they are in it, and they can definitely tell you when they are out of it. That is why I call being "in the zone" a paradoxical situation. A paradox exists when there is phenomena that is contradictory, but the conflicting information is not mutually exclusive. For the golfer "in the zone" the contradictory patterns are: 1) the golfer feels that s/he is "in control" and, at the same time, s/he senses that they are "out of control" 2) the golfer feels that "s/he can make no mistake", and yet, they cannot explain why they are so consistently "playing at such a peak performance level." Golfers in this state of mind are not thinking about the game and they are playing their very best.

As wonderful as it is, it is still a mystery how playing "in the zone" happens and the person who is experiencing this euphoric high in playing the game cannot explain how it happened and certainly cannot explain how long it will last. No one can play the game at such a peak level for too long. It may last for just a few holes, for a round, or for a tournament. Sometimes a professional golfer can go on a kind of "in the zone" binge that lasts for much of a golf season, but this is extremely rare.

I would wish for all of my readers and students to experience the golfing bliss of playing "in the zone." I cannot promise you that you will ever experience the transcendent high of playing golf "in the zone," but if you do, you will know the ineffable joy of playing a game that can light your life in ways that no other sport can.

STRETCHING EXERCISES

In order to make the proper movements in the Swing Formula, it is imperative to have flexibility throughout your body. The following exercises can help you to attain the necessary flexibility to enjoy your golf.

"The Windmill"

Address an imaginary golf ball with both arms fully extended (no golf club in your hands). Keeping your left arm fully extended and pointing at the imaginary ball, extend the right arm back until your arm has stretched back above your head. (Figures 60 & 61)

Figure 60   Figure 61

Both arms, when fully extended, should be in line with each other. The movement of your legs and hips in this exercise should be identical to the movement in the Swing Formula. Try to keep your head perpendicular to the imaginary ball. Now "windmill" your arms so that the right arm is pointing at the imaginary ball and the left arm is above your head. The arms will again be in line with each other. Try to keep your head perpendicular and your feet flat on the ground. Now bend your left arm and pivot to your right toe, bringing the right arm up to the left arm as if you have just completed the golf swing. Finish with the balance of weight on the outside of the left foot and heel. Link your hands together in an interlocking grip. (Figures 62 & 63) Perform this drill a couple of times before you start hitting balls and you will be ready to begin.

Figure 62   Figure 63

"Cross Wrist"

Extend both arms fully and set up in your address position. Cross your wrists with the right hand in front of the left. The right wrist must be below the left wrist. The back of each hand should be touching each other. (Figures 64, 65, & 66)

Figure 64   Figure 65

59

Figure 66

Now take your normal golf swing. This exercise should stretch your left side in the backswing for a full upper body rotation.   (Figures 67 & 68)

Figure 67   Figure 68

Acknowledgements

A very special thanks to David Sims for his contributions in the writing and editing of this book, especially for his ideas and contributions to the chapter "Secrets to Unlocking the Mental Part of the Game". He is a gifted writer, and having his great perspective, his years of experience and his understanding of the game of golf have been invaluable to me in preparing this book.

I would like to also thank Jerry P. Honstein for all of his efforts and contributions in the writing of this book. Many of his ideas, suggestions, and writing skills have helped me with this project.

All of the pictures in this book were taken at the historic Old Brockway golf course in Kings Beach, California. The photo number fifty three in this book was taken by the famed photographer Kiwi Kamera. All other pictures were taken by Fong Ying Cardy.

David Sims grew up in Douglas, Georgia, and began playing golf at an early age on a golf course that Bobby Jones helped to re-design. The entire Sims family were golf enthusiasts and his father co-sponsored an outstanding (winning) golfer on the PGA Tour.

Dr. Sims attended Duke University and Florida State University and his professional career was in college and university teaching (psychology and higher education) and administration. He served as President of a community college in Dallas, Texas, and Chancellor of a multi-college system in California.

Dr. Sims met Dave Cardy in Marin County, California, where Dave (at the time) held several course scoring records and was working as a professional golf instructor. They became close friends, played in tournaments together, taught golf together, and spent many hours sharing their ideas about the challenge of consistently playing outstanding golf. Dr. Sims became very impressed with Dave Cardy's Swing Formula instructional system for training beginners and experienced golfers. When he was asked to join Dave Cardy in writing Excellence in Golf, he enthusiastically accepted.

About Dave Cardy, Dr. Sims had this to say: "Dave Cardy has an amazing understanding of the game of golf - its history, the evolution of the equipment, the design and manufacture of the clubs, etc. - but the most important part of the game that Dave has mastered is the mechanics of the golf swing, and he has captured his depth of understanding of the essential steps to the golf swing in this book. Anyone who desires to improve their game and play consistent golf can do that by mastering Dave's Swing Formula sequence and applying his clearly-defined mechanics to their game. By applying Dave's concepts of the Swing Formula, any golfer can master the elements of the swing - and with swing mastery, the challenging mental part of the game will follow. With swing confidence and consistency, anyone can enjoy the game of golf and succeed on any golf course in the world."